Weight Watchers New Complete Cookbook 2022

Amanda Norman

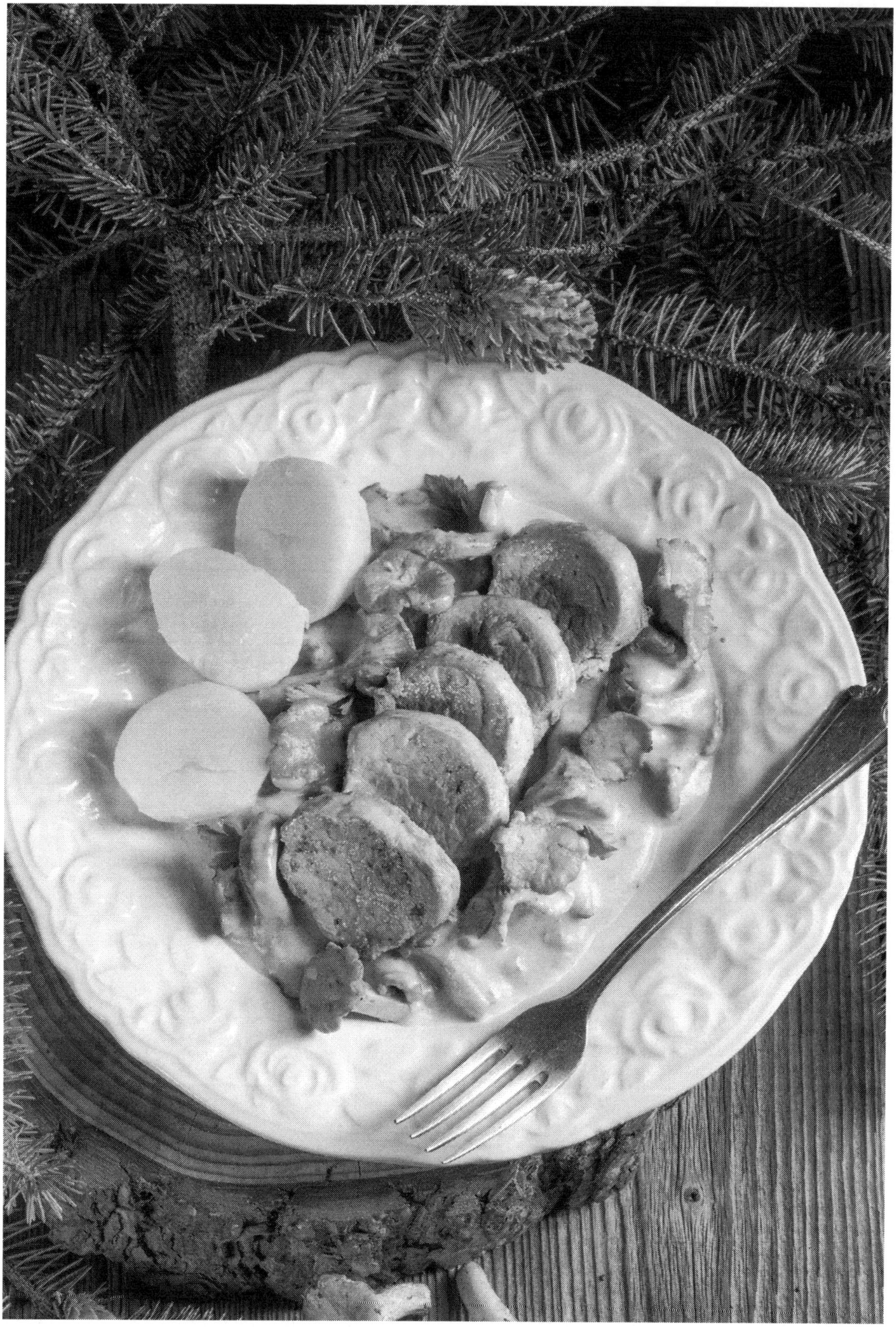

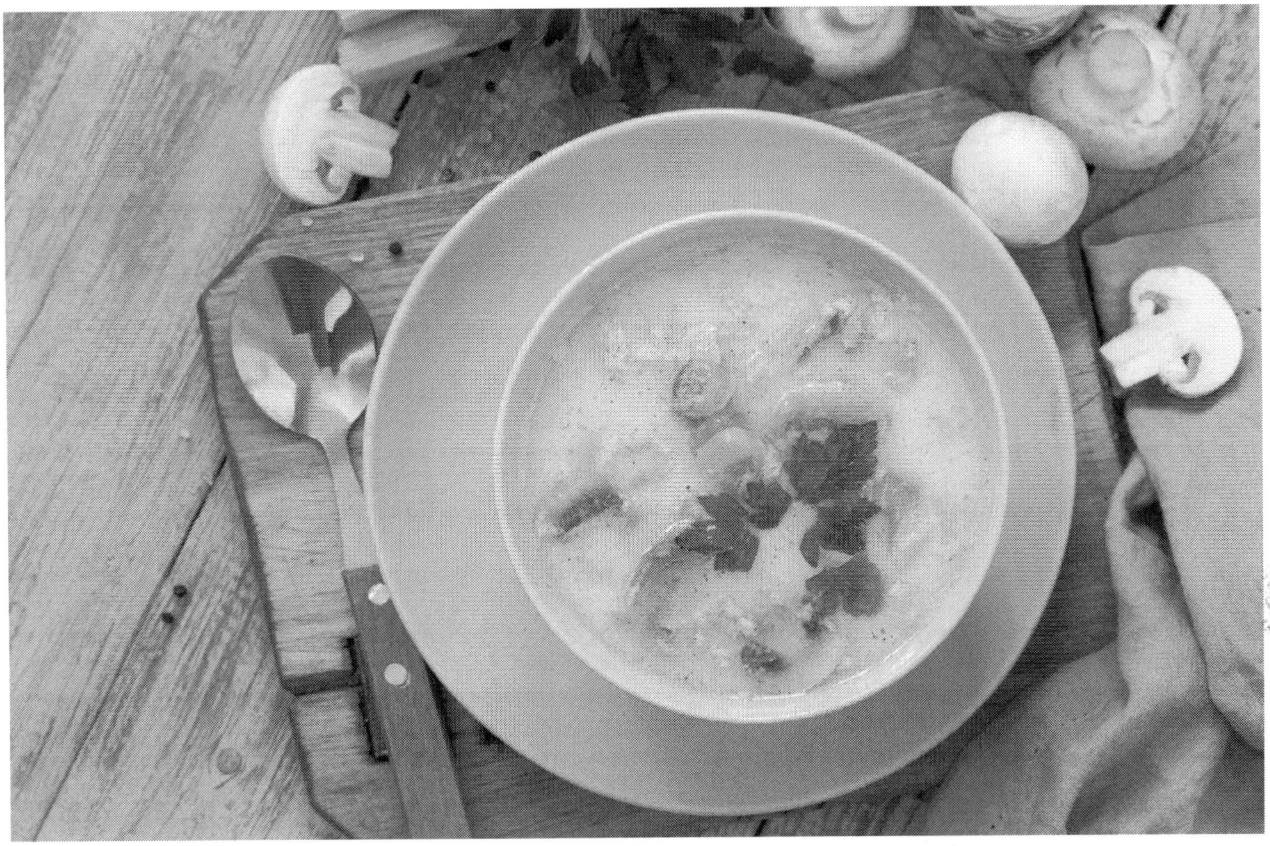

Copyright © 2022 - All rights reserved.

This document is geared towards providing exact and reliable information in regards to the topic and issue covered. The publication is sold with the idea that the publisher is not required to render accounting, officially permitted, or otherwise, qualified services. If advice is necessary, legal or professional, a practiced individual in the profession should be ordered.

From a Declaration of Principles which was accepted and approved equally by a Committee of the American Bar Association and a Committee of Publishers and Associations.
In no way is it legal to reproduce, duplicate, or transmit any part of this document in either electronic means or in printed format. Recording of this publication is strictly prohibited, and any storage of this document is not allowed unless with written permission from the publisher. All rights reserved.

The information provided herein is stated to be truthful and consistent, in that any liability, in terms of inattention or otherwise, by any usage or abuse of any policies, processes, or directions contained within is the solitary and utter responsibility of the recipient reader. Under no circumstances will any legal responsibility or blame be held against the publisher for any reparation, damages, or monetary loss due to the information herein, either directly or indirectly.

Respective authors own all copyrights not held by the publisher.

The information herein is offered for informational purposes solely and is universal as so. The presentation of the information is without a contract or any type of guarantee assurance.

The trademarks that are used are without any consent, and the publication of the trademark is without permission or backing by the trademark owner. All trademarks and brands within this book are for clarifying purposes only and are the owned by the owners themselves, not affiliated with this document.

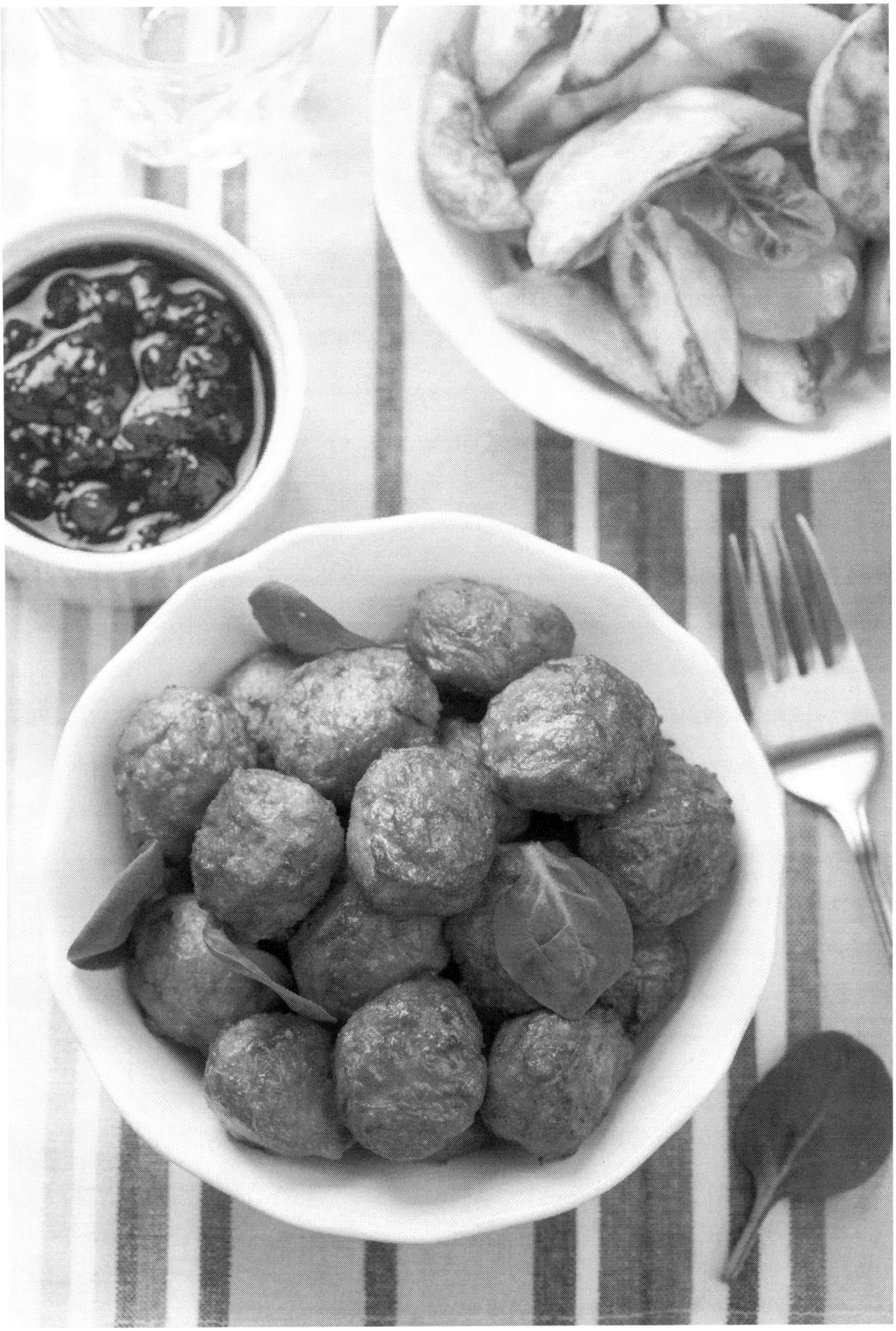

Contents

INTRODUCTION 9

CHAPTER 1: AN OVERVIEW OF WEIGHT WATCHERS 10
- What Is WW And What's Up With The Rebranding? 10
- What Happens When You Sign Up For WW? 11
- What Is myWW+? 12
- How Much Does WW Cost? 13
- How Do WW Plans Vary? 14
- What Are WW Zero Point Foods? 14
- Difference Between Weekly And Daily Smart Points 15
- Is The New Weight Watchers Program Effective? 16

CHAPTER 2: TOP TIPS FOR YOUR WEIGHT WATCHERS JOURNEY 17
- Organize Your Pantry 17
- Find Weight Watcher Certified Foods At Walmart 17
- Keep Yourself Hydrated 18
- Discover New Foods With The Zero Points System 18
- Add A Bit Of Zing 19
- Refresh Your Pantry 19
- Make Use Of The WW App 19
- Incorporate Workout 20
- Don't Worry Too Much 20
- Be More Social 20

CHAPTER 3: DECIDING IF WEIGHT WATCHERS IS RIGHT FOR YOU 21
- Weight Watcher Success Stories 21
- Can You Devote 15 Minutes A Day To Track Your Progress? 21
- Can You Workout Weekly? 22
- Do You Need Meetings? 22
- Can You Devote 30 Minutes A Day Of Physical Activity? 22
- Give The Program Few Weeks 23

CHAPTER 4: POTENTIAL BENEFITS AND DRAWBACKS OF WEIGHT WATCHERS PROGRAM 24
- This Is No Junk Science 24
- Weight Regain Is A Possibility 25
- Social Aspect Can Help With Motivation 25
- The Program Is Facilities By Coaches As Opposed To Medical Practitioners 25
- Weight Watchers Is Very Flexible 26
- The Lack Of Specificity Might Be A Problem 26

CHAPTER 4: UNDERSTANDING THE SMART POINTS SYSTEM 27
- What Are SmartPoints And How Do They Work? 27
- Personalized Plans 28

    Knowing About The Zero Points 28
    Common Ingredients SP 29
    Ingredients With Zero Point 33

CHAPTER 5: BREAKFAST RECIPES 36

    Orzo with Grilled Eggplant and Red Pepper 36
    Spanakopita Triangless 38
    Couscous with Lime and Scallions 40
    Bok Choy-Noodle Soup 41
    Herbed Couscous Pilaf 42
    Delicious Green Smoothie 44
    Warm Betty Oats 45
    Awesome Pumpkin Pie Oatmeal 46

CHAPTER 6: MEAT RECIPES 47

    Asparagus And Chicken Delight 47
    The Original Greek Lemon And Chicken Soup 48
    Chicken and Black Bean Chili 49
    Wheat Berries with Smoked Turkey and Fruit 51
    Herbed Up Roast Beef 53
    Exotic Korean Ham On A Stick 54

CHAPTER 7: SNACKS AND APPETIZERS 55

    Crispy Fried Apples 55
    Easy Scrambled Egg 56
    Curried Basmati Rice 57
    Smoked Flatbreads 58
    Baby Romaine With Clementine And Pecans 59
    Summery Pasta with Chickpeas and Tomatoes 60
    Summer Pasta And Chickpeas 61

CHAPTER 8: VEGAN AND VEGETARIAN 62

    Excellent Avocado Medley 62
    Refreshing Banana Smoothie 63
    Crunchy Delicious Soy Mix 64
    Caramelized Garlic Toasts 65
    Roasted Vegetable Crostini 66
    Ham Bruschetta And Portobello 67
    Perfect Italian Stuffed Mushrooms 68
    Roasted Kale Chips 70
    Watermelon Peach Salad And Ricotta 71

CHAPTER 9: FISH AND SEAFOOD 72

    Shrimp Scampi 72
    California Seafood Salad 73
    Lobster Salad 75
    Tuna and White Bean Salad 77
    Miso-Glazed Salmon 78
    Garlic Flavored Lemon Mahi Mahi 79

- Parm Garlic Shrimp 80
- Shrimp And Cilantro Platter 81

CHAPTER 10: DESSERTS 82
- Spiced Double Berry Crisp 82
- Chocolate-Espresso Mousse Shots 84
- Watermelon Sorbet 85
- Creamy Chocolate Mousse 86

CONCLUSION 88

Introduction

Many factors could be contributing to your recent increase in body weight if you believe you have gained weight recently. First, it is possible that the extra pounds were gained due to an unbalanced dietary intake that included an excessive amount of fatty foods that were high in calories. That is why it is critical to consult a weight watchers point list before beginning your diet.

Point lists can serve as a useful reference for what is recommended by experts around the world. In addition, they can assist you in optimizing your diet.

You can find a variety of meal recipes that have been specifically designed to ensure that you do not leave the dinner table hungry while at the same time allowing you to accurately manage the number of calories that you consume because they have been thoroughly tested before being made available to you.

To accomplish this, using a weight watchers point list can be extremely beneficial in figuring out how to shed some pounds. Many free weight watchers point lists can be found on the internet, and the majority of these lists have been created by people who have had personal experience with losing weight and reducing calorie intake.

Those concerned about their diet enough to alter what is served at the table will find the information in these lists extremely useful in their decision-making process. Weight watchers point lists include a variety of foods ranging from desserts to main dishes.

It is not always easy to refrain from indulging in your favorite foods. However, be careful not to deprive yourself of too many of your favorite foods; you can still find some on a weight watchers point list that is nutritious.

Although it is recommended that you refrain from eating them regularly, a treat every now and then will not harm you. Consult with an expert on the subject who can assist you in creating a list of foods to eat and foods to avoid, in addition to weight watcher point lists, to ensure that your diet is successful.

This way, you can tailor your diet to precisely meet your body's needs and watch the pounds melt away while still enjoying your favorite foods. Using weight watchers point lists is an absolute must when embarking on a weight-loss journey!

Chapter 1: An Overview Of Weight Watchers

Weight loss is a difficult endeavor. Weight gain, no matter how slow it may be, is so simple that you may not even be aware that it is taking place. When you wake up the next morning, you're the heaviest you've ever been in your life. That's what happened to me, at the very least. Unwanted weight gained due to mindless eating and leading a sedentary lifestyle was the cause of my gaining excess weight. It took me about a year or so to realize that I did not want to be in such pain any longer. Physically, I wasn't feeling well, and my clothes didn't seem to be fitting quite right. That's when I decided to turn to WW (formerly Weight Watchers). I lost 30 pounds in the first year of using the program, and I've maintained that weight loss ever since.

What Is WW And What's Up With The Rebranding?

A weight-loss program that has been in existence for 56 years, Weight Watchers (WW) rebranded itself in 2018, no doubt to avoid the stigma of being "your grandmother's diet." Weight Watchers' "new" program, dubbed "WW," is more a lifestyle program than a diet program. Nowadays, the most important goal is not simply to reach a specific number. Yes, losing weight is a beneficial side effect of the medication. However, it is more about assisting people in changing their bad habits and ultimately becoming healthier individuals, regardless of the number of people involved. Furthermore, it must be doing something right because people are raving about it. The success stories have piqued my interest as a millennial.

WW makes use of a simplified calorie-counting system that is personalized based on your age, weight, height, and gender to assist you in losing weight healthily and sustainably. The app or website allows you to keep track of everything you eat and drink, as well as your workouts. Depending on your goal, you are allotted a specific number of "SmartPoints" each day, accumulated over a week. With SmartPoints, every food and drink has a corresponding SmartPoint value. The healthiest foods are freebies that require no points at all—basically, it's calorie counting with significantly less complicated math. When it comes to SmartPoints, saturated fat and sugar are the biggest drivers, while protein is the biggest drag. The goal is to guide you toward making better decisions and, with time and repetition, to make those decisions second nature. Weight loss should be expected in theory if you consume the equivalent of your daily SmartPoints (or less than that number) and keep track of your progress on the WW platform once a week.

What Happens When You Sign Up For WW?

When you sign up, you'll be asked a series of questions about your lifestyle, eating habits, goals, level of activity, and so on. Because of the three color-coded programs available, the results of this personal assessment suggest the food values and total points you'll be working with, depending on which of the three color-coded programs you choose.

The Purple plan has more than 300 zero-point foods to choose from, but it also has the lowest number of total daily points of any of the plans. Therefore, in the Purple plan, you can reduce the amount of tracking by focusing on eating any of the 300 zero-point foods available to you. It does, however, hold you accountable for anything that isn't on the zero-point list, such as cocktails or the occasional cheeseburger, and you have fewer total points to spend as a result of this.

You will have the fewest zero-point foods (just over 100) on the Green plan, but you will have the highest number of daily points. Thus, while using Green, you're essentially tracking everything that you eat (or you're following a particularly boring diet). Still, you have a greater number of daily points at your disposal.

The Blue plan provides you with more than 200 zero-point foods and a moderate number of daily SmartPoints to choose from. A combination of flexibility and guidance is ideal for someone seeking a balance of both. This is the one that I selected.

What Is myWW+?

WW will launch a new program called myWW+ in November 2020, which will be available to all members. A brand-new assessment is available to WW members, including more in-depth questions about your lifestyle, habits, and goals. It takes a more comprehensive approach to weight loss, taking into account food and other factors that influence your health, such as your mindset and sleeping patterns. Additionally, it provides new tools to assist you in your health-related endeavors.

- New "What's in Your Fridge" meal planner suggests meals based on what you already have in your fridge or pantry.
- A more in-depth progress report that evaluates your progress both on and off the scale.
- An improved activity dashboard, which includes a new way to view FitPoints, encourages you to move more and discover workouts that you will enjoy help you move more and find workouts you will enjoy
- Short audio lessons are delivered through a new 5-minute coaching tool to assist with stress-eating management and finding motivation.
- New personalized recipes based on your food preferences are being developed.

Using science-based strategies, new sleep tools are being developed to assist you in getting to bed on time and getting a better night's sleep (my personal favorite new feature)

How Much Does WW Cost?

When you sign up, you will have the option to choose from a number of different plans. You pay by the week for each, with a minimum commitment of one month required—after all, healthy weight loss does not happen overnight (unfortunately).

It costs $3.83 per week (or approximately $15 to $19 per month) for the Digital plan, which gives you access to a more self-guided program and the app and the website. From there, you have access to food and fitness tracking features, as well as recipes and fitness guides, as well as a social platform where you can interact with other members and share your successes and frustrations with one another.

The Digital 360 plan ($5.07 per week, or approximately $20 to $25 per month) provides you with the same digital access as the Digital Access plan, as well as live and on-demand expert-led video content.

Choosing the Unlimited Workshops + Digital plan ($7.15 per week, or approximately $28 to $36 per month) provides you with digital access to Weight Watchers' programs as well as unlimited face-to-face (virtual or in-person) Coach-led sessions with other members (the famous meetings that were Weight Watchers' hallmark before the rebranding).

The 1-on-1 Coaching + Digital plan (not shown above) ($11.08 per week, or approximately $44 to $55 per month) provides you with digital access as well as private coaching to support you and your accountability if you require it.

If something comes up and you need to ask a question, you have access to a digital coach (also known as an online chat function) around the clock with all plans.

How Do WW Plans Vary?

Before I had my most recent success, I had attempted and failed to maintain a weight loss program. I began the 1-on-1 Coaching + Digital plan shortly after the beginning of the new calendar year. Additionally, it provided me with access to the digital platform in addition to personal coaching over the phone. I knew people on the WW program and were pleased with it, so I decided to join them. I managed to stick with it for about two months, but I didn't lose the weight I wanted, or at the rate I had hoped. While I was in this phase, I had a weekly 15-minute phone conversation with a WW coach. My coach was a pleasant and intelligent individual. Still, I did not find conversing with a complete stranger particularly beneficial. Who is this person who has approached me and inquired as to how many times I've been to the gym this week? To be honest, I could have chosen a different coach, and perhaps I would have had more success with someone who had a better personality match. In theory, I can see the advantages of having someone else motivate and hold you accountable for your actions. However, I needed to find motivation within myself rather than from outside sources.

Forward one year, and I've rejoined WW, this time on the less expensive Digital plan rather than the traditional plan. It may have come as a surprise to you that I made a weight-loss resolution for the New Year.) Unlike the last time, I stayed with it and lost 30 pounds, and I'm still at it. A more self-guided experience that focused on simple food tracking and mindful eating proved to be the most beneficial to my overall health and weight loss. It had a significant impact on my life by teaching me to eat more mindfully and intentionally. When it comes to eating healthy, I've made significant improvements, such as cutting back on junk food and increasing my intake of fruits and vegetables.

At first, the food tracking was time-consuming, but it soon became less time-consuming and more efficient. As an added bonus, I concentrated on zero-point foods, which reduced the amount of time I spent entering data into the app—I'm not sure if this is exactly the er, point of depriving healthy foods of any loggable value, but it worked for me. After a while, it became second nature to track down targets. WW also offers additional incentives known as "WellnessWins" to encourage people to maintain a consistent level of wellness. Since beginning the program, I've kept meticulous records and amassed over 12,000 WellnessWins (yes, yet another type of point) that I've used to purchase items such as a cookbook, new socks, and a sleeping mask.

What Are WW Zero Point Foods?

As previously stated, the number of zero-point foods varies depending on which program you choose, ranging from approximately 100 to more than 300. Overall, zero-point foods include most fruits and vegetables, eggs, lean proteins (chicken breasts, 99 percent lean ground turkey, most fish), and low-fat dairy products (such as yogurt).

Zero-point beverages contain no added sugar or fat, such as black coffee, black tea, and plain old water. In addition, there are a variety of diet beverages available that are zero points in value. (I have a soft spot for Diet Snapple.)

Difference Between Weekly And Daily Smart Points

The WW creators are well aware that if people do not have access to any of the high-point foods they crave, they are more likely to abandon their weight-loss efforts. So to compensate for this extra weekly point allocation, in addition to the daily points (which are intended to help keep you on track when you're trying to decide between a piece of steak (5 points on the Blue plan) and a piece of chicken (chicken breasts are 0 points), you're assigned an additional number of weekly points, also known as "weeklies."

Here's a little (poorly guarded) insider's tip: Working out, which earns you "FitPoints," can help you stretch your daily food budget a little further. For example, a half-hour of elliptical training at a high intensity produces approximately 9 FitPoints. In comparison, a half-hour of vigorous yoga produces 4 FitPoints. If you earn enough FitPoints, you'll be able to have more food points added to your daily SmartPoint budget if you reach a certain threshold. However, you are under no obligation to apply your FitPoints to your food plan if you do not wish to. Personal preference: having a set number of SmartPoints each week so that I don't accidentally overeat due to a misunderstanding of my FitPoints tracking is more comfortable for me. As an alternative, I chose to set a weekly FitPoint goal, which motivates me to work out by chasing that goal each week and allows me to compete against myself by increasing my activity. You can even sync devices with your WW apps, such as your phone or fitness tracker, to have the app track your activity for you automatically.

Becoming a member provides you with free access to do-it-anywhere fitness content through FitOn and Aaptiv, as well as hundreds of workouts on the WW blog that are available to the general public. FitOn is an online workout platform that provides free digital workouts that can be accessed directly from the WW app. Some of the benefits of FitOn include the fact that the workouts do not require any equipment and that many of the workouts are taught by celebrities. In addition, with the help of Aaptiv, you can create personalized audio-only workouts that are led by professional trainers.

Is The New Weight Watchers Program Effective?

I'm living proof that it is possible. However, the keyword here is "can." You must put in the effort and be willing to make some sacrifices. If you don't adhere to the plans to the letter or if you "cheat" excessively, you are only cheating yourself. When I concentrate on zero-point foods and keep track of everything, I can lose weight. When I deceive myself and track fewer points than I actually consume, I fail to make any significant progress. Having said that, simply maintaining one's weight is a significant accomplishment in and of itself. After a few years of using WW, I haven't noticed any significant weight gain since this journey. As a result, my weight will fluctuate from time to time due to the lessons that the WW lifestyle has instilled in me. Still, I've learned how to avoid completely sabotaging myself because of the lessons that the WW lifestyle has instilled in me.

I've lost a total of 30 pounds in total. In addition to transforming my physical appearance, this program assisted me in transforming my overall lifestyle and attitude toward food. I'm much more aware of what I'm putting into my body these days. I'm more conscious of how healthy (or unhealthily) certain foods or ingredients are (or aren't). It assists me in making better decisions when faced with the decision between one meal and a healthier alternative. Most of the time, I decline unhealthy foods, which is something I was not doing previously and which contributed to my weight gain in the first place. Because I put forth the necessary effort, it has completely transformed my life.

Even if you decide that you don't want to continue to pay for this program indefinitely, my experience has been that it is a fantastic starting point for a lifelong journey of caring for your body. I don't intend to use it indefinitely, but I appreciate that it is helping to keep me in check for the time being. However, once you have internalized how and why it works, you will be able to maintain your healthy habits long after you have completed this program—or, of course, you can return if you need a refresher.

Chapter 2: Top Tips For Your Weight Watchers Journey

When you first start out, it can be both exhilarating and overwhelming at the same time, but this is normal. There is SO much to learn, and your diet will evolve on a day-to-day basis as you progress. So I thought I'd share some quick and easy pointers to get you started on the right foot!

Organize Your Pantry

To start with a clean slate, you'll want to go through your refrigerator and pantry and see what you currently have on hand. Believe me when I say that it's difficult to keep any tempting foods on hand! Therefore, it's a good idea to write or label the points value per serving on top of any items you plan to keep.

Find Weight Watcher Certified Foods At Walmart

Whenever I'm out shopping and come across a product that has the Weight Watchers logo on it, it means I've discovered something new.

There are two varieties of JOLLY TIME® Healthy Pop® popcorn available, both of which are only 3 SmartPoints® for the entire bag of popcorn! I enjoy making one in the evenings for a filling and simple snack.

The Brownberry® Sandwich Thins rolls, which are endorsed by Weight Watchers®, have always been a personal favorite, even before I became a participant. I use them frequently for breakfast sandwiches, as burger buns, and a quick grilled sandwich for lunch. You can even cut them into wedges and bake them to make crackers with them!

Flatout® Flatbread, which is endorsed by Weight Watchers®, is available in various flavors, and I'm always coming up with new ways to use them! They range from 2-4 SmartPoints®, which is incredible considering how filling and high fiber. Many applications for these flatbreads include flatbread pizzas, baked taco cups, and even grilled wraps.

Keep Yourself Hydrated

It becomes a habit once you get used to carrying a water bottle around with you and drinking fluids regularly. If plain water becomes too monotonous, experiment with flavors such as lemon, mint, fruit, or sparkling water. I use my fitness tracker to keep track of how much water I've consumed throughout the day.

Discover New Foods With The Zero Points System

I have a list of zero-point items printed out and kept in my refrigerator and purse as a reference. I enjoy turning to it, particularly when I'm low on points and hungry or looking for a nutritious snack.

In preparation, eggs are extremely versatile; from hard-boiled to even a quick omelette, they make for a delicious snack or can be used to spice up a meal!

Increase the amount of fiber in your diet by including fruits and vegetables in everything. Peppers, cucumbers, and spinach are always staples in my sandwiches, always piled high with vegetables.

Please remember to include frozen items in your shopping list. They can be less expensive and more convenient to store.

Increase your intake of fish—shrimp and tuna are both delicious options for dinner!

Grilled chicken can be cut into cubes and stored in the refrigerator for a quick post-workout snack.

Add A Bit Of Zing

Look for spice blends that are salt-free to use on vegetables, salads, and meat. Don't forget to include some fresh herbs in your meal! This is an excellent time of year to experiment with growing your own small herb garden on your windowsill...

Refresh Your Pantry

Replace your high-point salad dressings with lower-point dressings made from yogurt or sugar-free varieties to save calories and points. Because I enjoy spicy foods, I always reach for sriracha or hot sauce, usually low in calories and fat. Greek yogurt is a fantastic substitute for sour cream, and it can be used to make delicious dips and dressings.

Make Use Of The WW App

You already spend time on it daily, so familiarize yourself with all of its benefits! I enjoy discovering new recipes and foods to incorporate into my weekly meal plan. After scanning a food item, click on the little star in the corner to add it to your favorites, which will save you time. It is extremely beneficial! When I cook a meal at home, I create a recipe in My Recipes and save it there.

Incorporate Workout

Even if it's only a matter of parking a little further away, getting out and about will benefit you. It is entirely up to you whether or not to make use of your activity points! I sync my fitness tracker with the app to see how many activity points I've accrued so far.

Don't Worry Too Much

When you're just getting started, you need to be gentle with yourself! For example, we went on vacation, and I tried to stick to the schedule, but I also wanted to have a good time. Then, I remembered that a meal was just that: a meal... (hello, beach drinks) I remembered that a meal was just that... After that, it was simply a matter of getting back on track. In the words of Aaliyah, "dust yourself off and start over." It is a new way of life rather than a diet.

Be More Social

Many wonderful people out there on social media share Weight Watchers products, meal ideas, and other information with others. Furthermore, being open and honest about your weight-loss journey can actually help to inspire you. So make a big deal about it! Follow the hashtag #WeightWatchers on Instagram or Twitter to learn some great tips and tricks and meet new people.

Chapter 3: Deciding If Weight Watchers Is Right For You

SlimFast, Paleo, and Keto, to name a few diets. Unfortunately, every diet I've tried either eliminates entire food groups (such as fruits!) or simply does not provide enough calories to keep me satisfied for long periods. Weight Watchers is a great program for people who enjoy eating and don't want to be restricted to a particular food group.

Almost everyone in the Weight Watchers (now Wellness that Works) community will tell you that Weight Watchers is a good fit for them, and for the most part, they are correct. Weight Watchers is an excellent program that many people have found to be successful – both for short periods and for the rest of their lives.

Weight Watcher Success Stories

Have you tried and failed at other diets in the past? I know I have in the past. Not sure about you, but if you tell me I can't have something, it only makes me want it that much more! Weight Watchers is not a diet; rather, it is a way of living. Even though it is cliche, it is true. Weight Watchers is a program that can be followed for the rest of your life – without feeling deprived. Not only that, but it's also a fun, healthy, and delicious alternative to the roller coaster diets that we've all tried in the past. I mean, I'm looking for something long-term. I'm looking for nutritious, delicious food that won't leave me hungry or deplete my body with essential vitamins and minerals.

Can You Devote 15 Minutes A Day To Track Your Progress?

You are not required to count calories or macronutrients, so don't stress... However, you must keep track of your points. I promise you that it will take you no more than fifteen minutes per day to complete this task. And, yes, you can set aside 15 minutes per day to track your progress. Whatever you set your mind to, you are capable of achieving. Weight Watchers has an app that makes it simple and enjoyable, and it can even make losing weight fun. My meals are prepared on Sundays and stored in containers for the following week. So that I am always aware of how many points I am consuming and when I label the containers with the point value of the meals. You are not required to do this, but I have found that doing so helps me keep track of the points I consume. 15 minutes a day can lead to a new, healthier, and slimmer version of yourself. So you're pressed for time and have a church, kids, and cleaning to complete on Sunday before the start of the workweek. I understand what you're saying. As a result, meal preparation must be simple and quick while still being nutritious and delicious. See these quick and easy InstantPot Weight Watchers meals that will have your meals ready in minutes.

Can You Workout Weekly?

Weight Watchers requires you to weigh in once a week to track your progress. You can join either online or in-person, depending on your preference. Both have their advantages. You'll want to be able to keep track of your accomplishments. Second, you want to see the weight fall off your body and reveal the new, lean, and mean version of yourself. Weekly weigh-ins allow you and your family to celebrate your accomplishments while keeping you motivated and on track.

Do You Need Meetings?

While attending Weight Watchers meetings is not required, doing so can significantly increase your chances of losing weight and maintaining it. Attendance at Weight Watchers meetings, according to some members, is essential to their weight loss success. Accountability, dependability, friendship, coaching, and celebrations of all successes are all provided during the meetings. Many of us have had great success with Weight Watchers as online members only, so if money is an issue, don't be afraid to sign up for an online membership first before trying to join in person.

Can You Devote 30 Minutes A Day Of Physical Activity?

Even though exercise isn't technically required for Weight Watchers' success, it certainly helps! Taking a brisk 30-minute walk 5 times a week will suffice to get you started on your fitness journey. However, the University of Pittsburgh researchers recommend that you get 40 minutes of exercise 5 times a week at the very least. A healthy body necessitates the consumption of nutritious foods as well as regular physical activity. These two things go hand in hand. Although weight loss can occur without exercise, it will occur much more quickly. You will be able to keep it off for the rest of your life if you follow a healthy exercise routine in conjunction with the Weight Watchers eating program. Here are some pointers on how to get 10,000 steps in a day.

Give The Program Few Weeks

You may not see immediate results at the beginning of your Weight Watchers journey, especially if you're already eating well and exercising. On the other hand, Weight Watchers is not a diet, so you must think about the long term. Setting realistic goals, such as a realistic goal weight, a specific dress size, or a specific pants size, will help you stay motivated and achieve the weight loss and body transformation you desire.

Chapter 4: Potential Benefits And Drawbacks Of Weight Watchers Program

Weight Watchers has been around for long, long before the paleo, keto, and South Beach diets. Weight Watchers, which was established in 1963, has outlasted a slew of fad diets and remains a popular program. The fact that the company is worth millions of dollars is also noteworthy.

The program works primarily by converting calories, saturated fat, sugar, and proteins into a simplified "points" system, encouraging participants to eat more nutritious foods, control portion sizes, and achieve a calorie deficit by eating fewer calories.

Several doctors and nutritionists were contacted to provide their professional opinions on Weight Watchers. As a result, it was discovered that the program has both advantages and disadvantages. Continue reading to discover what the experts want you to know before joining Weight Watchers or other diet programs.

This Is No Junk Science

The fact that Weight Watchers is "realistic," according to Dr. Dennis Gage, MD, FACP of Park Avenue Endocrinology and Nutrition, is something he appreciates.

"They don't use nonsense diets that consist solely of vitamins, injections, or potentially dangerous substances that could land a person in trouble," he explained. "It is effective if you follow the instructions."

Diet and exercise are the program's primary focus, rather than any miracle product or extreme regimen. And, although the science of health is constantly evolving, the benefits of tracking what Weight Watchers controls (calories, sugar, and so on) have been well-supported for many years.

Perri Halperin, a registered dietitian at Mount Sinai Hospital, explained to INSIDER that, while the Weight Watchers program has undergone revisions and updates over the years to stay current with nutrition trends and research, the basic premise has remained the same: a focus on healthy food choices, portion control, physical activity, nutrition education, and community support – all of which promote positive lifestyle change.

Weight Regain Is A Possibility

In the case of Weight Watchers, "someone may participate and do well for a number of months, but only 11 percent of those who participate are successful" in not regaining a significant amount of their body weight, according to Gage.

In his remarks, he was careful to point out that this is not a problem unique to Weight Watchers. However, like with any diet program, if a person's eating habits are not changed permanently, progress is highly likely to be halted or even reversed.

Social Aspect Can Help With Motivation

Gage cited the meetings and coaching that Weight Watchers provides as a positive aspect of the program.

As he explained, "It meets once a week, which means there's regular face-to-face contact with the coach." He added that human contact can aid in accountability and encourage participants to stick with it. Suppose you're thinking about joining Weight Watchers. In that case, it might be worthwhile to include in-person meetings as part of your overall strategy for success.

The Program Is Facilities By Coaches As Opposed To Medical Practitioners

According to Gage, the organization is not run by physicians. "Instead of physicians, you have coaches," he explained. For example, someone who wants to get the most bang for their buck will consult with a nutritionist or dietitian.

According to him, working with a medical professional has numerous advantages, including providing broader-spectrum care, the authority to prescribe medication if necessary, and the availability of additional tools for keeping patients on track.

When patients begin to gain weight again, Gage's practice, for example, uses an app that notifies doctors immediately so that they can address the situation quickly and effectively. It is possible to cancel your Weight Watchers membership, but it is more difficult to ghost a doctor.

Weight Watchers Is Very Flexible

Lisa Moskovitz of the New York Nutrition Group, a registered dietitian who works in the city, says that "compared to many other popular diets circulating in the media, Weight Watchers is superior in that it allows flexibility and encourages followers to eat plenty of plant-based [foods like] fruits and vegetables." Weight Watchers has been around since 1956.

In contrast to other weight-loss programs that emphasize cutting out unhealthy foods, the program emphasizes learning healthy eating skills such as portion control that will be useful even after you stop participating. Registered dietitian Laura Manning of Mount Sinai says she has had great success with Weight Watchers in educating patients about healthy eating habits for the rest of their lives.

"With the widespread availability of prepared foods, it can be difficult for a dieter to gauge the appropriate portion size because these meals can be substantial, to put it mildly," she told INSIDER. "These meals can be substantial, to put it mildly." Therefore, weight Watchers provides a " model " to better understand portion control for weight loss and long-term weight maintenance, Weight Watchers provides a "model."

The Lack Of Specificity Might Be A Problem

The plan, according to Moskovitz, can be "too lenient" for some people because it does not require a daily balance of different food groups, according to INSIDER. While the plan may encourage you to eat healthfully, it is still possible to consume a large amount of processed, low-nutrient food without exceeding your allotted point total.

According to Moskovitz, "many Weight Watchers members rely far too heavily on their meals and food products, which can prevent them from consuming more whole plant-based foods instead."

Aside from that, people who have specific health concerns to address may require more guidance than the program and its non-physician coaches are capable of providing.

According to Moskovitz, relying solely on a point system may not be sufficient for those who require more specific guidelines or are concerned about their blood sugar or cholesterol levels.

Chapter 4: Understanding The Smart Points System

The act of eating is one of life's greatest pleasures. It provides us with nourishment and aids in our ability to maintain our strength. Therefore, there should never be a time when anyone goes hungry. Therefore, we do not believe that any food should be prohibited.

When it comes to the World War II program, nothing is off the table. Upon registration, you will be provided with a personalized SmartPoints Budget, which you can use in the manner that best suits your preferences. You'll also be provided with tools that allow you to track your SmartPoints quickly and easily throughout the day.

Eating more healthfully has been shown to improve one's overall quality of life. Because of the straightforward SmartPoints system and the user-friendly WW app, not only does it taste delicious, but it's also easier than ever to prepare.

What Are SmartPoints And How Do They Work?

To make nutrition science more understandable, we created SmartPoints. These points are intended to assist you in developing a more nutritious eating pattern in your everyday life.

When you consume a food or drink, the SmartPoints system assigns it a point value, a single simple, precise number that is easy to remember and use. The point value is calculated based on the number of calories, saturated fat, sugar, and protein in the food or drink.

Increased sugar and/or saturated fat content in foods results in higher SmartPoints values. In contrast, increased lean protein content results in lower SmartPoint values.

As soon as you sign up for WW, you'll be given a SmartPoints Budget, which you can use in any way you choose.

Due to pre-calculated SmartPoints values, when you search for a food item in the WW app, the SmartPoints value will appear alongside the item in question. So all that is required is that you track, which is a very straightforward process.

Depending on your device, the app can be obtained free from the Apple App Store and the Google Play store.

Personalized Plans

WW will provide you with a personalized SmartPoints Budget at your initial registration, which will take into account your current body weight, height, gender, and age.

An additional weekly allowance (also known as your weeklies) is added to each day's budget. This additional money can be used for splurges such as larger portions or going out to dinner with friends. More information about your SmartPoints budget can be found by clicking here.

If you have SmartPoints that you are not planning to use right away, you can save them. SmartPoints will automatically roll over into your weekly SmartPoints balance if you have a new total of up to four daily SmartPoints. Those weeklies can be used whenever and however you want during the week, with no restrictions.

Knowing About The Zero Points

And the best news of all is that WW recognizes hundreds of ZeroPoint foods that do not require you to measure or track your intake.

ZeroPoint foods are exactly what they sound like - they are foods that have no SmartPoints value attached to them whatsoever. Why? These nutritional powerhouses serve as the foundation for a healthy eating pattern.

Despite not measuring or tracking your food, you can still lose weight by consuming ZeroPoint foods. This is because they are less likely to be overindulged than other foods.

As a result, even if you only have a few SmartPoints to spend, you'll always have something delicious to eat.

Common Ingredients SP

Below is a list of the most common ingredients alongside their associated Smart Point for your convenience.

Food with 0 SP

- Coffee
- Banana
- Apple
- Strawberries
- Chicken Breast
- Salad
- Blueberries
- Grapes
- Tomatoes
- Watermelon
- Egg White
- Lettuce
- Deli Sliced Turkey Breast
- Baby Carrots
- Orange
- Cucumber
- Broccoli
- Water
- Green Beans
- Pineapple
- Corn On The Cob (medium)
- Cherries
- Cantaloupe
- Spinach
- Fresh Fruit
- Raspberries
- Shrimp
- Asparagus
- Celery
- Cherry Tomatoes
- Carrots

- Yogurt
- Peach
- Sweet Red Potatoes
- Pear
- Salsa
- Tuna
- Diet Coke
- Mushrooms
- Onions
- Black Beans
- Blackberries
- Zucchini
- Grape Tomatoes
- Mixed Berries
- Grapefruit
- Nectarine
- Mango
- Mustard

Food with 1 SP

- Sugar
- Almond Milk
- Egg
- Guacamole
- Half and Half
- Salad Dressing

Food with 2 SP

- Cream
- Avocado
- 1 Slice Of Bread
- Scrambled Egg with milk/ butter
- Luncheon Meat, deli-sliced or ham (2 ounces)
- 2 t tablespoon of Hummus

Food with 3 SP

- Milk Skimmed
- 1 tablespoon of Mayonnaise

- Chocolate Chip Cookies
- Sweet potatoes ½ a cup
- 3 ounce of boneless Pork Chop
- 1 ounce of flour Tortilla
- Italian Salad Dressing 2 tablespoon
- 3 slices of cooked Turkey Bacon
- 1 cup of Cottage Cheese
- An ounce of crumbled feta

Food with 4 SP

- Olive Oil
- American Cheese 1 slice
- Low Fat Milk 1%, 1 Cup
- Cheddar Cheese 1 ounce
- Red Wine 5 ounce
- ¼ cup of Almond
- 5 ounces of White Wine
- Tortilla Chips 1 ounce
- Shredded Cheddar Cheese
- 1 tablespoon of honey
- 102 ounce of English Muffin
- Mashed Potatoes

Food with 5 SP

- Butter
- 3 Slices of Cooked Bacon
- Reduced Fat Milk 1 Cup
- Cooked Oatmeal 1 cup
- Plain Baked Potato, 6 ounce
- Regular Beer, 12 ounce
- 1 cup of cooked regular/ whole wheat pasta
- Hamburger Bun
- Ranch Salad Dressing
- Any type of Bagel (2 ounces)
- 1 cup of Spaghetti

Food With 6+ SP

- White Rice (6)

- Brown Rice (6)
- Peanut Butter 2 tablespoon (6)
- 1 Whole Cup Of Milk (7)
- 20 ounces of French Fries (13)
- 1 cup of cooked Quinoa (6)

Ingredients With Zero Point

- Peas such as chickpeas, sugar snap peas, black-eyed, etc.
- Beans such as black beans, kidney beans, pinto beans, fat-free refried beans, soybeans, sprouts, etc.
- Lentils
- Corn such as baby corn, sweet corn, corn on the cob
- Skinless Chicken Breast
- Skinless Turkey Breast
- Tofu
- Egg and Egg Whites
- Fish and Shellfish
- Yogurt
- Lean Ground Beef
- Non Fat and Plain Greek Yogurt
- All Fruits
- All Vegetables

To give you a more detailed look at the list, the following now hold a 0 SmartPoint value.

- Yogurt
- Plain Yogurt
- Greek Yogurt
- Watermelon
- Watercress
- Water Chestnuts
- Stir-Fried Vegetables
- Mixed Vegetables
- Sticks of Vegetables
- Turnips
- Turkey Breast
- Turkey Breast Tenderloin
- Ground Turkey Breast
- Tomato
- Tomato Sauce
- Tofu
- Taro
- Tangerine
- Tangelo
- Star fruit
- Winter and Summer Squash
- Spinach

- Shellfish
- Shallots
- Scallions
- Sauerkraut
- Chicken Satay
- Sashimi
- Salsa
- Salad
- Lentils
- Lime
- Lettuce
- Litchi
- Mangoes
- Mung Dal
- Mushroom Caps
- Nectarine
- Okra
- Onions
- Orange
- Parsley
- Pea Shoot
- Peaches
- Pear
- Pepper
- Pickles
- Pineapple
- Plums
- Pomegranate Seeds
- Pomelo
- Pumpkin
- Pumpkin Puree
- Radish
- Salad Mixed Greens
- Salad Three Bean
- Lemon Zest
- Leek
- Kiwifruit
- Jicama
- Jerk Chicken Breast
- Jackfruit
- Heart of Palm
- Guava

- Mixed Baby Greens
- Ginger Root
- Grape Fruit
- Fruit Cup
- Fruit Cocktail
- Fish Fillet
- Fruit
- Fish
- Figs
- Fennel
- Escarole
- Endive
- Egg Whites
- Eggs
- Apples
- Arrowroot
- Applesauce
- Artichoke
- Artichoke Hearts
- Bamboo Shoots
- Banana
- Beans
- Beets
- Blueberries
- Blackberries
- Broccoli
- Brussels
- Cabbage
- Carrots
- Cauliflower
- Cherries
- Chicken Breast
- Clementine
- Cucumber
- Dragon Fruit
- Egg Substitute
- Dates

And a few more.

Chapter 5: Breakfast Recipes

Orzo with Grilled Eggplant and Red Pepper

Number of Servings: 8

Prep Time: 10 minutes

Cooking Time: 8 minutes

Smart Points: 3

Ingredients:

- 6 ounces orzo
- 8 pitted kalamata olives, coarsely chopped
- 2 scallions, sliced
- 1 large tomato, seeded and chopped
- 1 small eggplant (about ¾ pound), cut into ½ inch rounds
- 1 small red bell pepper, quartered lengthwise and seeded
- ½ cup feta cheese, diced and fat-free
- 1 tablespoon olive oil, extra-virgin
- ¼ cup dill snipped fresh
- ¼ cup fresh parsley, chopped
- 1 lemon zest, grated
- ¼ teaspoon black pepper

Method:

1. Read package directions and cook orzo accordingly
2. You can skip the salt and drain
3. Take a serving bowl and transfer
4. Spray grill rack with nonstick spray
5. Preheat grill to medium, then spray eggplant with nonstick spray
6. Place eggplant and bell pepper on grill rack and grill for 4 minutes per side
7. Cut eggplant and bell pepper into ½-inch pieces
8. Add to orzo along with all remaining ingredients
9. Toss to mix well
10. Serve and enjoy!

Nutritional Values (Per Serving)

- Calories: 134
- Fat: 3 g
- Carbohydrates: 22 g
- Protein: 5 g
- Saturated Fat: 1 g
- Sodium: 182 mg
- Fiber: 3 g

Spanakopita Triangless

Number of Servings: 4

Prep Time: 15 minutes

Cooking Time: 25 minutes

Smart Points: 4

Ingredients:

- 2/4 cup crumbled reduced-fat feta cheese
- 1 (10-ounce) package frozen chopped spinach, thawed and squeezed dry
- 3 scallions, chopped
- ¼ cup snipped fresh dill
- 1 large egg white
- ¼ teaspoon black pepper
- 8 (9 x 14-inch) sheets frozen phyllo dough, thawed
- 2 tablespoons unsalted butter, melted

Method:

1. Place oven rack in center of oven. Preheat oven to 3 75 °F. Spray baking sheet with nonstick spray.
2. With a fork, mash feta in a medium bowl. Add spinach, scallions, dill, egg white, and pepper, stirring until mixed well.
3. Lay 1 phyllo sheet on the work surface with the long side facing you (keep remaining phyllo covered with a damp paper towel and plastic wrap); spray with olive oil nonstick spray. Top with another phyllo sheet and lightly spray. Cut phyllo crosswise into 6 strips. Place scant 1 tablespoonful of spinach mixture at one end of each strip. Fold comer of phyllo up and over filling, then continue folding flag-style to form a triangle.
4. Arrange filled triangles on a prepared baking sheet. Repeat with remaining filling and phyllo sheets, making a total of 24 triangles. Lightly brush tops of triangles with melted butter. Bake until golden brown, about 25 minutes. Serve hot or warm.

Nutritional Values (Per Serving)

- Calories: 98
- Fat: 3 g
- Carbohydrates: 0 g
- Protein: 5 g
- Saturated Fat: 3 g
- Sodium: 268 mg
- Fiber: 0 g

Couscous with Lime and Scallions

Number of Servings: 6

Prep Time: 10 minutes

Cooking Time: 5 minutes

Smart Points: 3

Ingredients:

- 1 and ½ cups water
- 1 cup whole wheat couscous
- 1 teaspoon extra-virgin olive oil
- ½ teaspoon salt
- 1 red bell pepper, finely chopped
- 1 carrot, finely chopped
- 8 scallions, thinly sliced
- ¼ cup lime juice
- ¼ cup finely fresh parsley, chopped
- 1/8 teaspoon black pepper

Method:

1. Take a medium saucepan and add water
2. Bring water to boil
3. Add couscous, oil, and salt
4. Remove saucepan from heat; let stand until water is absorbed for 5 minutes
5. Fluff couscous with a fork
6. Add all remaining ingredients to a serving bowl
7. Add couscous and toss to mix well
8. Serve and enjoy!

Nutritional Values (Per Serving)

- Calories: 164
- Fat: 2 g
- Carbohydrates: 34 g
- Protein: 6 g
- Saturated Fat: 0 g
- Sodium: 206 mg
- Fiber: 6 g

Bok Choy-Noodle Soup

Number of Servings: 6

Prep Time: 10 minutes

Cooking Time: 4 minutes

Smart Points: 3

Ingredients:

- ½ pound baby bok choy, coarsely chopped
- 2 scallions, thinly sliced on diagonal
- 2 (14 and ½ -ounce) can chicken broth, reduced-sodium
- 4 ounces cellophane noodles
- 1 teaspoon Asian (dark) sesame oil
- 1 (12-ounce) package tofu, low-fat extra-firm, cut into 1/2-inch dice
- ½ bunch watercress, trimmed
- 2 tablespoons reduced-sodium soy sauce
- ½ teaspoon black pepper

Method:

1. Take a large bowl and add noodles and enough hot water
2. Cover it for 5 minutes and then drain
3. Use kitchen scissors and cut noodles into 3- inch lengths
4. Pour broth into a large saucepan and bring to boil
5. Add bok choy and simmer until wilted about 2 minutes
6. Add noodles and remaining ingredients 2 minutes more
7. Serve and enjoy!

Nutritional Values (Per Serving)

- Calories: 141
- Fat: 3 g
- Carbohydrates: 21 g
- Protein: 8 g
- Saturated Fat: 0 g
- Sodium: 526 mg
- Fiber: 2 g

Herbed Couscous Pilaf

Number of Servings: 6

Prep Time: 12 minutes

Cooking Time: 5 minutes

Smart Points: 4

Ingredients:

- 1 cup couscous, whole wheat
- 1 tablespoon fresh flat-leaf parsley, chopped
- ¼ cup red bell pepper, finely diced
- ¼ cup red onion, diced
- 1 and ¼ cups vegetable broth, reduced-sodium
- 1 teaspoon lemon zest, grated
- 1 tablespoon lemon juice
- 2 teaspoons olive oil
- 1 teaspoon fresh rosemary, chopped
- ½ teaspoon salt
- 1/8 teaspoon black pepper

Method:

1. Take a medium-sized skillet and add oil
2. Heat oil over medium heat
3. Add bell pepper and onion
4. Cook and keep stirring for 5 minutes
5. Add broth, salt, and black pepper and bring to boil
6. Add couscous
7. Remove saucepan from heat
8. Keep aside for 5 minutes, then fluff couscous with a fork
9. Stir in lemon zest and juice, parsley, and rosemary
10. Serve and enjoy!

Nutritional Values (Per Serving)

- Calories: 117
- Fat: 2 g
- Carbohydrates: 21 g
- Protein: 4 g
- Saturated Fat: 0 g

- Sodium: 286 mg
- Fiber: 3 g

Delicious Green Smoothie

Number of Servings: 2

Prep Time: 10 minutes

Cooking Time: Nil

Smart Points: 1

Ingredients:

- 1 cup berries, frozen
- ½ cup baby spinach leaves
- 1 medium banana, ripe and sliced
- 2 tablespoons water
- 2 tablespoons orange juice, fresh

Method:

1. Add all the listed ingredients into your blender or food processor
2. Blend until you get a smooth mixture
3. Allow it to cool in your fridge
4. Serve and enjoy!

Nutritional Values (Per Serving)

- Calories: 321
- Fat: 11 g
- Carbohydrates: 55 g
- Protein: 5 g
- Saturated Fat: 2 g
- Sodium: 64 mg
- Fiber: 6 g

Warm Betty Oats

Number of Servings: 2

Prep Time: 10 minutes

Cooking Time: Nil

Smart Points: 3

Ingredients:

- 1-ounce dry oats rolled
- 1 ounce fresh blueberries
- ½ medium banana
- ¼ cups fresh raspberry
- 2/3 cups skim milk
- 1 teaspoon Acai powder
- ¼ teaspoon vanilla bean extract

Method:

1. Take a jug and add Acai powder, vanilla, and milk into it
2. Whisk them well
3. Use a fork to mash up the banana and raspberries
4. Take an airtight container and add the milk mix, raspberry, banana, raspberry, blueberries, and oats
5. Close the lid properly
6. Allow it to cool in your fridge overnight
7. Serve and enjoy!

Nutritional Values (Per Serving)

- Calories: 305
- Fat: 16 g
- Carbohydrates: 37 g
- Protein: 10 g
- Saturated Fat: 4 g
- Sodium: 126 mg
- Fiber: 5 g

Awesome Pumpkin Pie Oatmeal

Number of Servings: 2

Prep Time: 10 minutes

Cooking Time: 10 minutes

Smart Points: 6

Ingredients:

- ½ cup pumpkin, canned
- 1 cup oats
- Mashed banana, as needed
- 2 teaspoons maple syrup
- ½ teaspoon pumpkin pie spice
- ¾ cup almond milk, unsweetened

Method:

1. Take a bowl and add banana, mash the banana
2. Add remaining ingredients except for oats into the bowl
3. Mix them well
4. Add oats and stir the whole mixture more
5. Transfer the mixture to a cooking pot and cook over medium heat
6. Serve and enjoy!

Nutritional Values (Per Serving)

- Calories: 264
- Fat: 4 g
- Carbohydrates: 34 g
- Protein: 7 g
- Saturated Fat: 1 g
- Sodium: 246 mg
- Fiber: 5 g

Chapter 6: Meat Recipes

Asparagus And Chicken Delight

Number of Servings: 3

Prep Time: 10 minutes

Cooking Time: 25-30 minutes

Smart Points: 3

Ingredients:

- 2 pounds chicken breasts, cut in half to make 4 thin pieces
- ½ pounds asparagus, trimmed
- 8 provolone cheese slices
- 4 tomatoes, sundried and cut into strips
- Salt and pepper to taste

Method:

1. Preheat your oven to 400 degrees F
2. Take a large sheet and grease it well
3. Arrange chicken breasts and asparagus on a sheet pan and top with sundried tomatoes
4. Season well with salt and pepper, transfer to the oven
5. Bake for 25 minutes
6. Top with provolone cheese slices
7. Bake for 3 minutes
8. Serve and enjoy!

Nutritional Values (Per Serving)

- Calories: 321
- Fat: 15 g
- Carbohydrates: 3 g
- Protein: 40 g
- Saturated Fat: 3 g
- Sodium: 400 mg
- Fiber: 1 g

The Original Greek Lemon And Chicken Soup

Number of Servings: 4

Prep Time: 15 minutes

Cooking Time: 30 minutes

Smart Points: 2

Ingredients:

- 2 cups chicken, chopped and cooked
- 2 cans chicken broth, fat-free
- 1 can cream chicken soup, fat-free
- 1 garlic clove, minced
- ¼ cup lemon juice
- 2 tablespoons parsley, snipped
- 2 medium carrots, chopped
- 2/3 cup rice, long-grain
- ½ cup onion, chopped
- ¼ teaspoon pepper, grounded

Method:

1. Take your cooking pot and add all the listed ingredients except rice and parsley
2. Season the mixture with salt and pepper
3. Transfer pot over medium-high heat and bring the mix to a boil
4. Stir in rice and lower heat to medium
5. Simmer for 20 minutes
6. Garnish with parsley
7. Serve and enjoy!

Nutritional Values (Per Serving)

- Calories: 591
- Fat: 33 g
- Carbohydrates: 31 g
- Protein: 32 g
- Saturated Fat: 8 g
- Sodium: 1356 mg
- Fiber: 2 g

Chicken and Black Bean Chili

Number of Servings: 4

Prep Time: 15 minutes

Cooking Time: 45 minutes

Smart Points: 5

Ingredients:

- 1 pound chicken breast, grounded and skinless
- 1 (28-ounce) can tomatoes, crushed
- 2 teaspoons olive oil
- 1 tablespoon chili powder
- 2 teaspoons ground cumin
- 1/8 teaspoon cayenne
- 1 (15 and ½ ounce) can black beans, rinsed and drained
- 2 red bell peppers, chopped
- 1 large onion, chopped
- 3 garlic cloves, minced

Method:

1. Take a large pot and add oil
2. Heat oil over medium heat
3. Add bell peppers, onion, and garlic and cook
4. Keep stirring until onion is softened about 5 minutes
5. Add chicken and cook for 7 minutes
6. Add tomatoes, chili powder, cumin, and cayenne to Dutch oven
7. Bring to boil
8. Reduce heat and simmer
9. Keep stirring for about 30 minutes
10. Stir in beans; simmer until heated through about 3 minutes longer
11. Serve and enjoy!

Nutritional Values (Per Serving)

- Calories: 316
- Fat: 6 g
- Carbohydrates: 34 g
- Protein: 32 g
- Saturated Fat: 1 g
- Sodium: 731 mg
- Fiber: 11 g

Wheat Berries with Smoked Turkey and Fruit

Number of Servings: 4

Prep Time: 5 minutes

Cooking Time: Nil

Smart Points: 6

Ingredients:

- 1 (½ pound) piece smoked turkey, diced
- 1 Granny Smith apple, peeled, cored, and diced
- 2 nectarines, pitted and cut into ½-inch pieces
- 1 cup wheat berries, rinsed
- 1 tablespoon Dijon mustard
- ½ (10-ounce) bag baby spinach, coarsely chopped
- ½ red onion, finely chopped
- ¼ cup orange juice
- 3 tablespoons cider vinegar

Method:

1. Take a large pot and add water
2. Bring to boil over medium-high heat
3. Stir in wheat berries
4. Reduce heat and simmer, covered, until berries are tender but still chewy, 45 minutes-1 hour
5. Drain and let cool
6. Take a large bowl and add wheat berries, turkey, nectarines, apple, and onion into it
7. Take a small bowl and add orange juice, vinegar, and mustard into it
8. Whisk them together to make dressing
9. Drizzle dressing over wheat berry mixture
10. Toss to coat evenly
11. Line platter with spinach, top with wheat berry mixture
12. Serve and enjoy!

Nutritional Values (Per Serving)

- Calories: 298
- Fat: 2 g
- Carbohydrates: 51 g
- Protein: 22 g
- Saturated Fat: 0 g
- Sodium: 105 mg
- Fiber: 9 g

Herbed Up Roast Beef

Number of Servings: 3

Prep Time: 10 minutes

Cooking Time: 1 hour and 10 minutes

Smart Points: 3

Ingredients:

- 1-pound rump roast, boneless
- ½ cup beef bone broth
- ½ teaspoon rosemary, dried
- 1 teaspoon parsley flakes, dried
- 1 tablespoon yellow mustard
- 4 garlic cloves, peeled and halved
- 2 yellow onions, quartered
- 1 teaspoon thyme, dried
- Salt and pepper to taste

Method:

1. Take a towel and pat your roast dry with your towel
2. Rub roast with mustard spices all over
3. Place rump roast in roasting pan and then pour beef broth
4. Scatter garlic and onions around the meat
5. Transfer to a pre-heated oven to 360 degrees F
6. Roast for 30 minutes and lower heat to 220 degrees F
7. Then roast for 30-40 minutes more
8. Serve and enjoy!

Nutritional Values (Per Serving)

- Calories: 316
- Fat: 13 g
- Carbohydrates: 2 g
- Protein: 47 g
- Saturated Fat: 4 g
- Sodium: 660 mg
- Fiber: 0.5 g

Exotic Korean Ham On A Stick

Number of Servings: 4

Prep Time: 10 minutes

Cooking Time: 10-15 minutes

Smart Points: 5

Ingredients:

- 1 teaspoon chili-garlic sauce
- 2 teaspoons Asian fish sauce
- 2 garlic cloves, minced
- 1 tablespoon fresh ginger, grated
- ¼ cup honey
- ¼ cup low sodium soy sauce
- ½ cup cider vinegar
- 6 scallions, chopped
- 1 and ¼ pound flank steak, sliced

Method:

1. Soak 16 (12-inch) wooden skewers in water for at least 30 minutes.
2. Thread steak onto skewers, dividing evenly; place in large baking dish. Stir together all remaining ingredients in a small bowl; pour over meat, turning to coat. Cover and refrigerate for at least 2 hours or up to 4 hours.
3. Spray broiler rack with nonstick spray and preheat broiler.
4. Drain marinade into a small saucepan; bring to boil. Boil, occasionally stirring, until sauce is thickened, about 8 minutes.
5. Meanwhile, place skewers on broiler rack and broil 5 inches from heat, turning, until meat is browned, about 4 minutes per side. Arrange skewers on a platter and drizzle evenly with sauce.

Nutritional Values (Per Serving)

- Calories: 145
- Fat: 1 g
- Carbohydrates: 9 g
- Protein: 16 g
- Saturated Fat: 0 g
- Sodium: 426 mg
- Fiber: 2 g

Chapter 7: Snacks And Appetizers

Crispy Fried Apples

Number of Servings: 4

Prep Time: 10 minutes

Cooking Time: 10 minutes

Smart Points: 1

Ingredients:

- 4 granny smith apples, peeled and cored
- ¼ cup date paste
- ½ cup coconut oil
- 2 tablespoons cinnamon, grounded

Method:

1. Take a large skillet and place it over medium level heat
2. Add oil and heat the oil
3. Add date paste and cinnamon into the hot oil
4. Then add apple slices to the mix
5. Cook for 5-8 minutes
6. Serve and enjoy!

Nutritional Values (Per Serving)

- Calories: 368
- Fat: 23 g
- Carbohydrates: 44 g
- Protein: 1 g
- Saturated Fat: 10 g
- Sodium: 182 mg
- Fiber: 12 g

Easy Scrambled Egg

Number of Servings: 2

Prep Time: 10 minutes

Cooking Time: 10 minutes

Smart Points: 2

Ingredients:

- 3 whole eggs
- 1 tablespoon butter, melted
- ½ cup feta cheese, crumbled
- 1 teaspoon water
- Salt and pepper to taste

Method:

1. Take a skillet and place it over medium level heat
2. Add butter and let it heat up, and melt
3. Take a bowl and add water, eggs, pour the mix into the pan
4. Whisk them well
5. Stir in feta cheese
6. Keep stirring gently until scrambled
7. Season with salt and pepper
8. Serve and enjoy!

Nutritional Values (Per Serving)

- Calories: 183
- Fat: 15 g
- Carbohydrates: 1 g
- Protein: 10 g
- Saturated Fat: 2 g
- Sodium: 200 mg
- Fiber: 1 g

Curried Basmati Rice

Number of Servings: 6

Prep Time: 10 minutes

Cooking Time: 25 minutes

Smart Points: 3

Ingredients:

- 1 cup basmati rice
- ½ red bell pepper, chopped
- ½ green bell pepper, chopped
- 8 cremini or white mushrooms, sliced
- 1 and ½ teaspoons curry powder
- 2 onions, chopped
- ¼ teaspoon salt
- 1 and ½ cups water

Method:

1. Take a large saucepan and spray it with nonstick spray
2. Place the pan over medium heat
3. Add mushrooms, onions, and bell peppers
4. Cook and keep stirring until softened about 5 minutes
5. Stir all remaining ingredients into vegetable mixture and bring to boil
6. Reduce heat and simmer, and cover it for about 20 minutes
7. Serve and enjoy!

<u>Nutritional Values (Per Serving)</u>

- Calories: 153
- Fat: 0 g
- Carbohydrates: 33 g
- Protein: 4 g
- Saturated Fat: 0 g
- Sodium: 102 mg
- Fiber: 3 g

Smoked Flatbreads

Number of Servings: 4

Prep Time: 15 minutes

Cooking Time: 10 minutes

Smart Points: 4

Ingredients:

- 2 teaspoons olive oil
- 1 tablespoon lemon juice
- 1 tablespoon capers, drained
- ¼ small red onion, sliced
- 2 cups lightly packed watercress sprigs
- 3 ounces thinly sliced smoked salmon
- 2 tablespoons fat-free milk
- 4 ounces light cream cheese
- 2 whole-grain lavash flatbreads

Method:

1. Preheat oven to 400°F. Spray a large baking sheet with nonstick spray.
2. Place lavash on a prepared baking sheet and bake until lightly browned and crispy, about 10 minutes.
3. Meanwhile, stir together cream cheese and milk until smooth. Spread cream cheese mixture over lavash. Top with salmon.
4. Place watercress, onion, capers, lemon juice, and oil in a large bowl and toss to coat. Top lavash with watercress mixture and cut each lavash into 8 pieces.

Nutritional Values (Per Serving)

- Calories: 184
- Fat: 2 g
- Carbohydrates: 1 g
- Protein: 7 g
- Saturated Fat: 1 g
- Sodium: 318 mg
- Fiber: 7 g

Baby Romaine With Clementine And Pecans

Number of Servings: 4

Prep Time: 15 minutes

Cooking Time: Nil

Smart Points: 2

Ingredients:

- 2 clementine, peeled and sectioned
- 6 cups lightly packed baby romaine lettuce
- ¼ teaspoon pepper
- ¼ teaspoon salt
- 2 teaspoons extra virgin olive oil
- 2 tablespoons orange juice
- 2 tablespoons pecans, chopped
- ¼ cup snippets fresh chives

Method:

1. To make the dressing, whisk together orange juice, oil, salt, and pepper in a small bowl until well blended.
2. Toss together romaine, clementines, chives, and pecans in a salad bowl. Drizzle dressing over and toss to coat evenly.

Nutritional Values (Per Serving)

- Calories: 78
- Fat: 1 g
- Carbohydrates: 7 g
- Protein: 2 g
- Saturated Fat: 1 g
- Sodium: 115 mg
- Fiber: 2 g

Summery Pasta with Chickpeas and Tomatoes

Number of Servings: 8

Prep Time: 5 minutes

Cooking Time: Nil

Smart Points: 6

Ingredients:

- 3 cups whole wheat pasta, such as Gemelli, shells, or elbows
- 2 celery stalks, sliced
- 1 (15 and ½-ounce) can chickpeas, rinsed and drained
- 1 each red and yellow tomato, seeded and diced
- ¼ cup parsley leaves, lightly packed fresh flat-leaf
- 2 tablespoons red wine vinegar
- 1/8 teaspoon red pepper flakes
- 1/3 cup feta cheese, coarsely crumbled reduced-fat
- 1 tablespoon olive oil
- ½ teaspoon oregano, dried
- ½ teaspoon salt
- ¼ teaspoon black pepper

Method:

1. Read package directions and cook accordingly
2. Skip the salt if you want
3. Drain in a colander and rinse under cold running water; drain again
4. Take a serving bowl and add pasta and all remaining ingredients except feta
5. Sprinkle with cheese
6. Serve and enjoy!

Nutritional Values (Per Serving)

- Calories: 200
- Fat: 3 g
- Carbohydrates: 37 g
- Protein: 9 g
- Saturated Fat: 1 g
- Sodium: 288 mg
- Fiber: 5 g

Summer Pasta And Chickpeas

Number of Servings: 4

Prep Time: 15 minutes

Cooking Time: Nil

Smart Points: 3

Ingredients:

- 3 cups whole wheat pasta
- 1 can chickpeas, rinsed and drained
- 1 red and yellow tomato, sliced and diced
- 2 celery stalks, sliced
- ¼ cup lightly packed fresh flat-leaf parsley leaves
- ½ teaspoon salt
- ½ teaspoon dried oregano
- 1 tablespoon olive oil
- 2 tablespoons red wine vinegar
- ½ cup coarsely crumbled reduced-fat feta cheese
- ½ teaspoon red pepper flakes
- ¼ teaspoon black pepper

Method:

1. Cook pasta according to package directions, omitting salt if desired. Drain in a colander and rinse under cold running water; drain again.

2. Toss together pasta and all remaining ingredients except feta in a serving bowl. Sprinkle with cheese.

Nutritional Values (Per Serving)

- Calories: 200
- Fat: 3 g
- Carbohydrates: 37 g
- Protein: 9 g
- Saturated Fat: 1 g
- Sodium: 288 mg
- Fiber: 3 g

Chapter 8: Vegan And Vegetarian

Excellent Avocado Medley

Number of Servings: 3

Prep Time: 10 minutes

Cooking Time: 5 minutes

Smart Points: 1

Ingredients:

- ½ avocado, chopped
- 3 ounces bacon, sliced
- 1 tablespoon almonds, chopped
- 1 teaspoon coconut milk
- 1 tablespoon lemon juice
- 1 cup arugula lettuce
- 1 teaspoon olive oil

Method:

1. Take your chopping board and chop sliced avocado roughly
2. Toss it in a skillet, then roast for 5 minutes
3. Once bacon becomes crunchy, add bacon to the salad bowl
4. Add chopped avocado, almonds to the bowl
5. Add coconut milk, olive oil, and lemon juice
6. Then mix them well to make a mixture
7. Pour dressing over salad and mix
8. Serve and enjoy!

Nutritional Values (Per Serving)

- Calories: 402
- Fat: 32 g
- Carbohydrates: 10 g
- Protein: 20 g
- Saturated Fat: 8 g
- Sodium: 243 mg
- Fiber: 2 g

Refreshing Banana Smoothie

Number of Servings: 2

Prep Time: 10 minutes

Cooking Time: Nil

Smart Points: 2

Ingredients:

- 2 cups kale, chopped
- 1 whole banana
- ½ cup light almond milk, unsweetened
- 1 tablespoon flax seed

Method:

1. Take your banana and chop it up
2. Add all of the listed ingredients into your blender
3. Blend until you get a smooth mixture
4. Serve and enjoy!

Nutritional Values (Per Serving)

- Calories: 311
- Fat: 7 g
- Carbohydrates: 56 g
- Protein: 12 g
- Saturated Fat: 3 g
- Sodium: 139 mg
- Fiber: 7 g

Crunchy Delicious Soy Mix

Number of Servings: 4

Prep Time: 15 minutes

Cooking Time: 5-10 minutes

Smart Points: 4

Ingredients:

- 1 tablespoon canola oil
- 3 tablespoons low sodium soy sauce
- ½ cup unsalted dry roasted peanuts
- 1 cup roasted soy sauce
- 1 cup unsweetened puff corn cereal
- 1 cup whole grain Cheddar crackers
- 1 cup rice cereal squares
- ½ teaspoon cayenne

Method:

1. Preheat oven to 3 7 5 °F.
2. Combine cereal squares, crackers, puffed corn, soy nuts, and peanuts in a large bowl. Combine soy sauce, oil, and cayenne in a small bowl. Add soy sauce mixture to cereal mixture and toss well. Spread on a large baking sheet.
3. Bake 5 minutes; stir and bake until lightly browned and crispy, 2 minutes longer. Cool completely; store in an airtight container for up to 1 week.

Nutritional Values (Per Serving)

- Calories: 121
- Fat: 1 g
- Carbohydrates: 10 g
- Protein: 5 g
- Saturated Fat: 0 g
- Sodium: 206 mg
- Fiber: 2 g

Caramelized Garlic Toasts

Number of Servings: 4

Prep Time: 15 minutes

Cooking Time: 12-15 minutes

Smart Points: 2

Ingredients:

- ½ cup water
- 1 tablespoon honey
- 12 large garlic cloves, peeled
- ¼ teaspoon cayenne Pinch salt
- Pinch black pepper
- 2 tablespoons unsalted butter, softened
- 8 thin slices of French bread, toasted

Method:

1. Combine water and honey in a small saucepan; bring to simmer over medium-low heat. Add garlic and cook until softened, about 12 minutes. Add cayenne, salt, and black pepper; cook until garlic turns deep golden, about 3 minutes.
2. Transfer garlic mixture to a mini food processor. Add butter and process until smooth. Serve with toasts.

Nutritional Values (Per Serving)

- Calories: 127
- Fat: 4 g
- Carbohydrates: 3 g
- Protein: 3 g
- Saturated Fat: 1 g
- Sodium: 210 mg
- Fiber: 1 g

Roasted Vegetable Crostini

Number of Servings: 4

Prep Time: 15 minutes

Cooking Time: 45 minutes

Smart Points: 4

Ingredients:

- 12 kalamata olives, pitted
- ½ cup fresh basil, chopped
- 8 ounces Italian bread, cut into 24 slices and toasted
- ½ teaspoon pepper
- ¾ teaspoon salt
- 1 teaspoon dried oregano
- 2 tablespoons extra virgin olive oil
- 1 onion, sliced
- 2 zucchini, chopped
- 2 red bell pepper, chopped
- 1 pound eggplant, cut into ½ inch dice
- ¼ cup parmesan cheese, grated

Method:

1. Preheat oven to 425 ° F.
2. Toss together eggplant, bell peppers, zucchini, onion, oil, oregano, salt, and black pepper in a large roasting pan. Spread to form a single layer. Roast vegetables, occasionally stirring, until tender and browned along edges, about 45 minutes. Let cool to room temperature.
3. Spoon vegetable mixture evenly onto toasts. Sprinkle evenly with basil, olives, and Parmesan.

Nutritional Values (Per Serving)

- Calories: 140
- Fat: 1 g
- Carbohydrates: 22 g
- Protein: 4 g
- Saturated Fat: 0.2 g
- Sodium: 417 mg
- Fiber: 2 g

Ham Bruschetta And Portobello

Number of Servings: 4

Prep Time: 15 minutes

Cooking Time: 5-10 minutes

Smart Points: 5

Ingredients:

- 2 tablespoons parmesan cheese, grated
- 2 (1 ounce) lean black forest ham, cut into half
- 2 teaspoons low soy sodium soy sauce
- 2 teaspoons extra virgin olive oil
- 1 garlic clove, halved
- 2 slices country bread, cut crosswise
- 4 large portobello mushroom stems removed

Method:

1. Spray grill rack with nonstick spray; preheat grill to medium or prepare the medium fire.
2. Lightly spray mushrooms with nonstick spray. Place on grill rack and grill until lightly browned and tender, about 5 minutes per side. Transfer to a plate.
3. Lightly spray both sides of slices of bread with nonstick spray. Place on grill rack and grill until golden brown, about 1 minute per side. Rub one side of each slice of bread with a cut side of garlic and drizzle evenly with oil.
4. Slice mushrooms and divide among slices of bread; drizzle evenly with soy sauce. Top each bruschetta with 1 piece of ham; sprinkle with Parmesan.

Nutritional Values (Per Serving)

- Calories: 107
- Fat: 1 g
- Carbohydrates: 2 g
- Protein: 6 g
- Saturated Fat: 0.5 g
- Sodium: 329 mg
- Fiber: 0.5 g

Perfect Italian Stuffed Mushrooms

Number of Servings: 6

Prep Time: 15 minutes

Cooking Time: 45 minutes

Smart Points: 5

Ingredients:

- ½ teaspoon black pepper
- ½ teaspoon salt
- ½ teaspoon dried oregano
- 1 large egg white
- ¼ cup romano cheese, grated
- ¼ cup plain dried bread crumbs
- ¼ cup fresh parsley, chopped
- 1 small onion, chopped
- 30 cremini mushrooms, stems chopped, and caps preserved
- ½ pound sweet Italian turkey sausages, casing removed

Method:

1. Preheat oven to 3 5 0°F. Spray jelly-roll pan with nonstick spray.
2. To make the mushroom filling, spray a medium skillet with nonstick spray and set it over medium-high heat. Add sausages and cook, breaking them apart with a wooden spoon until they are no longer pink, about 5 minutes. Add mushroom stems, onion, and garlic; cook, stirring, until mushrooms begin to brown, about 6 minutes. Transfer to a medium bowl and let cool for about 5 minutes.
3. Add all remaining ingredients to the sausage mixture, stirring to mix well. Spoon about 2½ teaspoons filling into each mushroom cap. Place stuffed mushrooms in a prepared pan. Bake until mushrooms are tender and filling is heated through about 20 minutes. Serve hot or warm.

Nutritional Values (Per Serving)

- Calories: 91
- Fat: 4 g
- Carbohydrates: 1 g
- Protein: 8 g
- Saturated Fat: 1 g
- Sodium: 366 mg
- Fiber: 8 g

Roasted Kale Chips

Number of Servings: 4

Prep Time: 15 minutes

Cooking Time: 20 minutes

Smart Points: 5

Ingredients:

- 1 tablespoon parmesan cheese, grated
- ¼ teaspoon pepper
- 1 tablespoon olive oil
- 8 cups lightly packed baby kale

Method:

1. Preheat oven to 3 2 5 °F.
2. Spray 2 large rimmed baking sheets with nonstick spray. Toss together kale, oil, salt, and pepper in a large bowl.
3. Spread in a single layer on prepared baking sheets. Roast, without stirring, until edges are lightly browned, and kale is crisp about 20 minutes.
4. Gently transfer to serving bowl; sprinkle with cheese and toss to coat evenly.

Nutritional Values (Per Serving)

- Calories: 104
- Fat: 5 g
- Carbohydrates: 14 g
- Protein: 5 g
- Saturated Fat: 1 g
- Sodium: 232 mg
- Fiber: 3 g

Watermelon Peach Salad And Ricotta

Number of Servings: 4

Prep Time: 15 minutes

Cooking Time: Nil

Smart Points: 3

Ingredients:

- ½ cup coarsely crumbed ricotta salsa
- ¼ teaspoon salt
- 3 tablespoons champagne vinegar
- 2 mini cucumbers
- 2 large peaches, pitted and cut
- 1 piece seedless watermelon, rind, and cut into ¾ inch dice

Method:

1. Take a bowl and toss everything in a serving bowl
2. Let the mix stand for 10 minutes
3. Sprinkle with scallion and cheese
4. Enjoy!

Nutritional Values (Per Serving)

- Calories: 133
- Fat: 5 g
- Carbohydrates: 19 g
- Protein: 4 g
- Saturated Fat: 2 g
- Sodium: 359 mg
- Fiber: 2 g

Chapter 9: Fish And Seafood

Shrimp Scampi

Number of Servings: 4

Prep Time: 7 minutes

Cooking Time: 5 minutes

Smart Points: 5

Ingredients:

- 1 and ¼ pounds medium shrimp, peeled and deveined, tails left on if desired
- ½ cup chicken broth, reduced-sodium
- 6 large garlic cloves, minced
- ½ cup dry white wine
- 4 teaspoons olive oil
- ¼ cup fresh parsley, finely chopped
- ¼ cup lemon juice
- ¼ teaspoon salt
- ¼ teaspoon black pepper

Method:

1. Take a medium-sized skillet and add oil
2. Heat oil over medium heat
3. Add shrimp and cook until just opaque in the center about 3 minutes
4. Add garlic and cook
5. Keep stirring for 1 minute
6. Use a slotted spoon to transfer shrimp into a platter
7. Add all remaining ingredients to skillet and bring to boil
8. Boil until sauce is reduced by half
9. Serve and enjoy!

Nutritional Values (Per Serving)

- Calories: 163
- Fat: 1 g
- Carbohydrates: 3 g
- Protein: 23 g
- Saturated Fat: 1 g
- Sodium: 467 mg
- Fiber: 0 g

California Seafood Salad

Number of Servings: 4

Prep Time: 5 minutes

Cooking Time: 5 minutes

Smart Points: 9

Ingredients:

- 1 cup croutons
- ½ pound cooked medium shrimp, peeled and deveined, tails left on if desired
- ¼ pound cooked crabmeat, picked over
- 12 cherry tomatoes, halved
- ½ avocado, pitted, peeled, and diced
- 4 cups red leaf lettuce, lightly packed torn
- 2 navel oranges, peeled and sectioned
- ¼ cup clam-tomato or tomato juice
- 1 tablespoon Worcestershire sauce
- ¼ cup lemon juice
- 4 teaspoons olive oil
- ¼ teaspoon salt
- ¼ teaspoon black pepper

Method:

1. Take a small bowl and add Worcestershire sauce, salt, clam-tomato juice, lemon juice, oil, and pepper into the bowl

2. Whisk them well to make dressing

3. Line platter with lettuce, mound crabmeat in center

4. Arrange shrimp, tomatoes, avocado, and oranges around crabmeat

5. Drizzle dressing over and scatter croutons on top

6. Serve and enjoy!

Nutritional Values (Per Serving)

- Calories: 261
- Fat: 10 g
- Carbohydrates: 23 g
- Protein: 22 g
- Saturated Fat: 1 g
- Sodium: 562 mg
- Fiber: 6 g

Lobster Salad

Number of Servings: 4

Prep Time: 7 minutes

Cooking Time: Nil

Smart Points: 4

Ingredients:

- 1 pound cooked lobster meat, cut into chunks
- 1 mango, peeled, pitted, and diced
- 2 cups lightly packed tender watercress sprigs
- 1 pink grapefruit, peeled, sectioned, and coarsely chopped
- ¼ cup orange juice
- 1 navel orange, peeled, sectioned, and coarsely chopped
- 1 and ½ cups cantaloupe balls
- 2 tablespoons fresh chives, snipped
- ½ cup sour cream, fat-free
- 3 tablespoons mayonnaise, reduced-fat
- 2 teaspoons orange zest, grated
- ¼ teaspoon salt
- ¼ teaspoon black pepper

Method:

1. Take a large bowl and add lobster, grapefruit, orange, cantaloupe, and mango into it
2. Mix well
3. Line platter with watercress; mound lobster salad on top
4. Take a small bowl and add all remaining ingredients except chives
5. Whisk together to make dressing
6. Spoon dressing over salad; sprinkle with chives
7. Serve and enjoy!

Nutritional Values (Per Serving)

- Calories: 291
- Fat: 8 g
- Carbohydrates: 31 g
- Protein: 26 g
- Saturated Fat: 3 g
- Sodium: 738 mg
- Fiber: 3 g

Tuna and White Bean Salad

Number of Servings: 4

Prep Time: 5 minutes

Cooking Time: Nil

Smart Points: 6

Ingredients:

- 1 (15 and ½-ounce) can cannellini (white kidney) beans, rinsed and drained
- 2 (5-ounce) cans of water-packed light tuna, drained and flaked
- ½ red onion, chopped
- 3 celery stalks, sliced
- ¼ cup fresh parsley, chopped
- 3 tablespoons lemon juice
- 2 garlic cloves, minced
- 2 teaspoons sage, dried
- 2 teaspoons olive oil
- ¼ teaspoon salt
- ¼ teaspoon black pepper

Method:

1. Take a serving bowl and add all ingredients
2. Mix them well
3. Serve and enjoy!

Nutritional Values (Per Serving)

- Calories: 180
- Fat: 3 g
- Carbohydrates: 15 g
- Protein: 22 g
- Saturated Fat: 1 g
- Sodium: 573 mg
- Fiber: 4 g

Miso-Glazed Salmon

Number of Servings: 6

Prep Time: 10 minutes

Cooking Time: 10 minutes

Smart Points: 8

Ingredients:

- 6 (5-ounce) skinless salmon fillets
- 3 tablespoons white miso
- 3 tablespoons brown sugar
- 2 tablespoons soy sauce, reduced-sodium

Method:

1. Take a large shallow baking dish and add miso, brown sugar, and soy sauce into it
2. Whisk them together
3. Add salmon and turn to coat
4. Cover and marinate in your refrigerator for 15 minutes
5. Preheat oven to 425 degrees F
6. Bake for 10 minutes.
7. Serve and enjoy!

Nutritional Values (Per Serving)

- Calories: 273
- Fat: 11 g
- Carbohydrates: 9 g
- Protein: 32 g
- Saturated Fat: 3 g
- Sodium: 566 mg
- Fiber: 1 g

Garlic Flavored Lemon Mahi Mahi

Number of Servings: 3

Prep Time: 10 minutes

Cooking Time: 30 minutes

Smart Points: 2

Ingredients:

- 4 pieces (4 ounces each) mahi-mahi fillets
- 3 garlic cloves, minced
- 1 lemon zest
- 1 tablespoon extra-virgin olive oil
- ½ teaspoon pepper

Method:

1. Take a skillet and place it over medium heat
2. Add oil and heat it
3. Add garlic and sauté for a few minutes
4. Add fillets and season with lemon zest and pepper
5. Preheat your oven to 350 degrees F
6. Transfer fish to the oven
7. Bake for 30 minutes
8. Serve and enjoy!

Nutritional Values (Per Serving)

- Calories: 111
- Fat: 2 g
- Carbohydrates: 2 g
- Protein: 21 g
- Saturated Fat: 1 g
- Sodium: 162 mg
- Fiber: 0.5 g

Parm Garlic Shrimp

Number of Servings: 4

Prep Time: 10 minutes

Cooking Time: 6-10 minutes

Smart Points: 4

Ingredients:

- 1 and ¼ pounds raw shrimp, peeled and deveined
- ¼ cup parmesan, grated
- 2 tablespoons olive oil
- 3 garlic cloves, minced
- 1 lemon juice
- 1 teaspoon Italian seasoning
- Salt and pepper to taste

Method:

1. Preheat your oven to 300 degrees F
2. Take your baking sheet and add shrimp, cheese, seasoning, garlic, olive oil
3. Toss well until nicely coated
4. Then transfer to your pre-heated oven
5. Cook for 6-8 minutes
6. Serve and enjoy!

Nutritional Values (Per Serving)

- Calories: 138
- Fat: 7 g
- Carbohydrates: 2 g
- Protein: 16 g
- Saturated Fat: 2 g
- Sodium: 644 mg
- Fiber: 1 g

Shrimp And Cilantro Platter

Number of Servings: 3

Prep Time: 10 minutes

Cooking Time: 5 minutes

Smart Points: 0

Ingredients:

- 1 and ¾ pounds shrimp, peeled and deveined
- 1 and ¼ cups fresh cilantro, chopped
- ¼ teaspoon cumin, grounded
- 1 tablespoon olive oil
- 1 teaspoon lime zest
- 2 tablespoons fresh lime juice
- ½ teaspoon salt
- ¼ teaspoon pepper

Method:

1. Take a large-sized bowl and add shrimp, cumin, garlic, lime juice, ginger
2. Toss them well
3. Take a large-sized non-stick skillet and add oil
4. Allow the oil to heat up over medium-high heat
5. Add shrimp mixture and sauté for 4 minutes
6. Remove the heat and add cilantro, lime zest, salt, and pepper
7. Mix well
8. Serve hot and enjoy!

Nutritional Values (Per Serving)

- Calories: 177
- Fat: 6 g
- Carbohydrates: 3 g
- Protein: 27 g
- Saturated Fat: 2 g
- Sodium: 650 mg
- Fiber: 2 g

Chapter 10: Desserts

Spiced Double Berry Crisp

Number of Servings: 6

Prep Time: 10 minutes

Cooking Time: 20 minutes

Smart Points: 7

Ingredients:

- 1 pint fresh blueberries
- 1/3 cup sugar, granulated
- 2 (6-ounce) containers of fresh raspberries or blackberries
- ½ orange, grated
- 1 tablespoon cornstarch
- ¼ teaspoon salt

Toppings:

- ½ cup old-fashioned rolled oats
- 1 tablespoon unsalted butter, melted
- 1 tablespoon canola oil
- ¼ cup white whole wheat flour
- 2 tablespoons light brown sugar
- ¼ teaspoon nutmeg, grounded
- 1 teaspoon cinnamon, grounded
- Pinch salt

Method:

1. Preheat your oven to 375 degrees F
2. Spray 1 and ½ -quart baking dish with nonstick spray
3. Take a large bowl and add all filling ingredients
4. Toss together all filling ingredients to make the topping, then spoon into baking dish
5. Take a medium bowl and add all topping ingredients
6. Stir together to make the topping
7. Squeeze the mixture together to form a loose ball, then break into small pieces and sprinkle evenly, overfilling
8. Bake for 20 minutes
9. Serve hot and enjoy!

Nutritional Values (Per Serving)

- Calories: 202
- Fat: 5 g
- Carbohydrates: 38 g
- Protein: 3 g
- Saturated Fat: 1 g
- Sodium: 146 mg
- Fiber: 5 g

Chocolate-Espresso Mousse Shots

Number of Servings: 16

Prep Time: 10 minutes

Cooking Time: 10 minutes

Smart Points: 2

Ingredients:

- 1 (1.4-ounce) package fat-free, sugar-free instant chocolate pudding mix
- 1 and ½ cups whipped topping, thawed, frozen, and fat-free
- 16 chocolate wafer cookies, broken into pieces
- 1 tablespoon hot water
- 2 teaspoons instant espresso powder
- 1 and ½ cups milk, fat-free

Method:

1. Take water and espresso powder in a cup
2. Stir together until espresso is dissolved
3. Allow it to cool at room temperature
4. To make the mousse, whisk together pudding mix and milk until combined well
5. Whisk in espresso, then fold in ½ cup of whipped topping
6. Line up 16 shot glasses
7. Spoon 1 tablespoon of mousse into each glass; top with 1 and ½ teaspoons of cookie pieces 1 and ½ tablespoons of mousse and 1 teaspoon cookie pieces
8. Add 1 tablespoon of whipped topping on top
9. Serve hot and enjoy!

<u>Nutritional Values (Per Serving)</u>

- Calories: 54
- Fat: 1 g
- Carbohydrates: 9 g
- Protein: 1 g
- Saturated Fat: 1 g
- Sodium: 123 mg
- Fiber: 0 g

Watermelon Sorbet

Number of Servings: 4

Prep Time: 10 minutes

Cooking Time: Nil

Smart Points: 3

Ingredients:

- 4 cups seedless watermelon chunks
- 2 tablespoons lime juice
- ¼ cup superfine sugar

Method:

1. Add all ingredients into your blender or food processor
2. Blend until you get a smooth mixture
3. Transfer to a freezer container with a tight-fitting lid
4. Freeze and cover it until mixture resembles set gelatin 4-6 hours
5. Puree watermelon mixture in batches into your blender or food processor
6. Cover it and freeze overnight
7. Serve at room temperature and enjoy!

Nutritional Values (Per Serving)

- Calories: 91
- Fat: 0 g
- Carbohydrates: 27 g
- Protein: 1 g
- Saturated Fat: 0 g
- Sodium: 5 mg
- Fiber: 1 g

Creamy Chocolate Mousse

Number of Servings: 16

Prep Time: 10 minutes

Cooking Time: 20 minutes

Smart Points: 6

Ingredients:

- 8 ounces bittersweet chocolate, chopped
- ½ cup orange slivers, candied
- ¼ cup egg whites, powdered
- ¾ cup warm water
- ½ cup sugar
- 3 tablespoons hazelnut liqueur

Method:

1. Take a medium saucepan and fill with 1 inch of water, then bring to simmer over medium heat
2. Put the chocolate in a medium bowl and set over simmering water
3. Cook and keep stirring until chocolate is melted and smooth, about 5 minutes
4. Remove bowl from the saucepan
5. Take a large bowl and combine chocolate and liqueur into it
6. Whisk together powdered egg whites and warm water until egg white powder is completely dissolved about 2 minutes
7. Beat egg white mixture until foamy with electric mixer on low speed
8. Increase speed to medium-high and beat until soft peaks form when beaters are lifted
9. Add 2 tablespoons sugar at a time, beating until stiff, glossy peaks form when beaters are lifted
10. Stir with a rubber spatula about one-third of the meringue into chocolate mixture
11. Fold remaining meringue into chocolate mixture in two batches just until whites are no longer visible
12. Spoon mousse into 16 dishes and refrigerate for at least 3 hours
13. Sprinkle with candied orange
14. Serve hot and enjoy!

Nutritional Values (Per Serving)

- Calories: 123
- Fat: 7 g
- Carbohydrates: 16 g
- Protein: 2 g
- Saturated Fat: 5 g
- Sodium: 9 mg
- Fiber: 2 g

Conclusion

People who are overweight can lose weight with the help of the Weight Watchers diet, which uses a point-counting system to assist them in their efforts. Keeping track of your food intake is essential for success, as each food item has a point value assigned to it. You must also ensure that you stay within your daily points budget to be successful. Given that high-calorie or empty-calorie foods consume more points than other foods restricting your intake of these foods will aid you in losing weight by lowering your overall energy intake.

However, this does not necessarily imply that the plan is the most advantageous option for all parties involved. While there are many positive aspects to Weight Watchers, it also can promote unhealthy dieting habits. While some people may find the constant tracking irritating, others may attempt to manipulate the points to gain an advantage (skipping meals to bank points for less healthy foods). It can also be extremely expensive for a long time.

According to the Weight Watchers program, you should expect to lose between 1 and 2 pounds per week if you follow the program's recommendations. To get started, Weight Watchers recommends that you first assess your current situation and determine how much weight you want to lose in the first week of membership. Then, measure your waist and hips during week 1 to compare your results later on in the program.

Made in the USA
Middletown, DE
19 December 2021